My Map
Of
Scars

Written by Sam Shaw

My Map of Scars- Sam Shaw

Prologue

I felt compelled to share my story with you, in hopes that it might reach someone who's struggling with feelings of loneliness or isolation, just as I once did. As a young girl, I faced deep pain, heart-ache, and an overwhelming sense of being alone in this world. But instead of reaching out for help, I kept everything bottled up inside, thinking I had to carry the weight on my own.

I want you to know, and I hope my story helps you realize — that keeping it all in was the worst thing I could have done.

If you're going through something similar, please, don't do what I did. Please seek out help, go talk to someone, whether it's friends, family, or a professional. Trust me, I could have lost my life because I didn't speak up, and I was lucky to make it through. You are not alone, and most importantly, the person who will always have your back, no matter what, is *you*.

Please, love yourself more — right now, at this moment. You deserve it!

This story is my way of reaching out, hoping to remind you that you can find strength, healing, and the courage to keep going.

My name is Sam Shaw. I was born in the late seventies. I was born three months premature, weighing one pound thirteen ounces. I was so tiny that I had to stay in an incubator for three months to reach a healthy weight of five pounds. I was in the neonatal intensive care unit before my mom could take me home from the hospital.

My parents were not married when I was born. When I was born, I had a few minor birth defects. I was born with cataracts and hypoglycemia. I was very lucky, considering some premature babies are born with much worse health issues, including heart and lung issues. In the late seventies in our area, there was not a lot of knowledge of hypoglycemia or infants born with cataracts. I had a really hard time seeing properly, and didn't know what clear vision was. I had many seizures because my blood sugar was too low. I was told I would have seizures weekly. We didn't have a doctor in town that was familiar with this condition. When a new doctor arrived, they understood the situation and its cause.

I spent a significant amount of time in the hospital until I was around six years old. I am currently in my late forties and have not experienced a seizure since that age. I am grateful every day that I don't ever have to deal with having a seizure again.

There was an occasion when my father took me to the hospital because my sugar levels were low. I was wearing a pink Winnie the Pooh overall outfit. My mother was at work, and my father had to go to work as well. I expressed distress because I did not want him to leave me alone. That is when I started to feel abandonment, but I don't know for sure.

My father was married when he met my mother. He then got divorced, and shortly after, I was born. They were married at the Justice of the Peace. I was three years old at the time and came down with chickenpox, so I did not attend their wedding.

CHAPTER

When I was about nine, my parents often attended late-night parties and had many friends who owned bars. One particular night, they went to party at a bar in the United States. It was just across the Canadian border, and they took me along to play with the bar owner's granddaughter. We slept in the same bed while the parents and grandparents had fun drinking and hanging out with their friends.

As I look back on it, I think it was a little crazy of my parents to do this, and I know it wasn't good for me, but back then; I didn't know any different. However, that was not the real issue I wanted to tell you about.

So, as I mentioned, my parents were at the bar and by now probably had a few too many drinks. A woman my dad worked with was sitting next to him and talking. My mom saw this from a distance and thought the woman was flirting with him. She became jealous, and because my dad had cheated on his first wife (*with my mom*), so she's automatically decided that he was being unfaithful to her and flew into a rage.

My mom left the bar and ran into my room yelling and screaming and had grabbed me out of bed. I was crying and scared because I had no idea what the heck was going on. We ran outside into the pitch-black night and pouring rain.

Standing in front of the car, my mom informed me, "Your father and I are over," and then asked, "Who do you want to live with? Me, or your father?"

"Dad," I replied.

She lost her shit! In a drunken rage she had taken me by the head and smashed my face into the hood of our car. I was crying, bleeding, and scared shitless because my mom was drunk and going to drive us home.

But as I said before, we were in the USA, so we had to go through the border to Canada to get back home. She instructed me not to look at the officer due to the bleeding from my lip and a laceration above my eye. Upon our arrival at the border, the officer did not inquire about our situation nor request that we enter the office for questioning. However, once we had crossed the border, my mother decided to return to the bar in the USA. Upon returning, she placed me back in bed, as if nothing happened.

The next morning, I had woken up with cuts on my face and a bruise from her smashing my face against the car. Both my parents acted like nothing happened.

Honestly, I had asked myself, did my parents love me back then or even one another? But I realized that they had issues that were not resolved. From that moment in time, I hated being alone with my mom. She would flip out for no reason at all, well not for any reason I knew of.

That life made me feel like things were very unpredictable for me and this created anxiety in me, which wasn't really something people talked about back in the mid-eighties. I was just a kid, but I knew how I had felt. My dad worked twelve-hour shifts, and because of his work rotation, he was home more than my mom. Dad and I played soccer and threw the ball around. I loved my dad so much. My mom worked days and was always stressed.

It was Christmas time I remember, and I had received an exceptional Christmas gift; my parents had adorned the Christmas tree with a Goofy character ornament that had a key attached to a ribbon. This key was intended to unlock my toy room. I was told I needed to find that key on the tree. It was a great memory as I recall it now, I was so excited. In my old toy room, there were tickets to Disney world, a computer, and tickets to go see New Kids on the Block *(NKOTB)* in concert. They were my favorite music band, and I had a huge crush on Joey Mc Intyre.

In February we went to Florida, and in March, we went to the NKOTB Concert! I went to see New Kids on the Block with my mom, Aunt Sandy, and babysitter Meg. Aunt Sandy did my hair and makeup. I wore a Levi's jean jacket and ripped red tab jeans. I felt so cool and happy! I will never forget what an amazing year that was.

CHAPTER

This was the year that I had become very close with my cousin, Jenny. We were inseparable, frequently having sleepovers. She resided in the east end of town, while I lived in the north end, our family home was beautiful.

At the beginning of the year, I started becoming interested in boys who were into skateboarding. I had decided, back then, that if I was into what they are into, they might like me more. So, my dad bought me a skateboard, not a really good one, but it was alright!

A boy in my class named Lucas had a skateboard for sale, he was asking eighty dollars for it. I told him my parents would consider buying it. He responded positively.

When I went home and asked, my dad said, "No, you already have one, and it might be unsafe."

I was disappointed and even offered to use my own allowance, but the answer was still no.

Despite me usually getting my requests met, this time it was different. I returned to school and informed Lucas that I wasn't allowed to have it. He laughed at me. So, I decided I would snoop around for money or a cheque at home. I found a blank cheque of my parents and the next day; I brought it over to Lucas and his buddy who helped me to forge my dad's name on the cheque.

I took the skateboard home and hid it in the garage. At around five pm that evening, there was a knock on the door. Lucas and his dad were there with the check in hand. Mom had just returned home. They handed the check to my mom, and I had to return the skateboard.

My mom expressed her anger and said, "Wait till your father gets home."

I went to my room and waited. My dad arrived at home shortly after seven pm. My mother explained my actions to my father. He then came into my room and expressed his disappointment in me, emphasizing the seriousness of what I had done. As a consequence, he grounded me for a month without access to my phone, friends, television, or any other fun activities. I completely understood the gravity of the situation, and my dad did not resort to any physical punishment.

Girls my age back then were-into makeup and diets. This particular diet trend I remember back then was an ice cube diet. Kids our age should not have been on a diet, but TV and peer pressure was our influence, much like today.

On this particular Saturday, my mother went shopping with friends, leaving my father at home with me. Jenny happened to call, and my father permitted me to speak with her. She was the only person I was allowed to communicate with. Jenny had asked if I could sleep over, so we planned it. I hoped my grounding would be over, and it was, I slept over at her place! *Yay!*

Jenny and I were really close back then. Our parents would play cards every weekend and have drinks. Even as the years passed, Jenny and I were still close, like sisters. My parents didn't have any more children and as an only child, to me she was always more like a sister than a cousin.

I played soccer once a week during the summer. I loved it, and I was pretty good! I was on a team of all boys. My dad would come to every game! He was so proud of me.

That year, Jenny and I were fifteen years old when my parents brought me and Jenny to Ottawa, Ontario. We went shopping on the Outdoor Market in the big city. We were so excited to be given that opportunity. We had walked around and seeing all the buskers, the restaurants, and people all dressed in a grunge style! Back then I felt like we were walking in heaven being able to go do that.

I vividly remember walking into a store called Neon where they sold Doc Martens. I wanted a pair with black eight holes! My parents bought them for me! My foot size was size one! Just to give you an idea of how small I was back then.

Jenny 's parents had given her some money, but it wasn't enough, this made Jenny a little jealous of me. But my parents decided to buy them for Jenny too and told her to keep her spending money on something special!

I remember Jenny was wearing a floral jumper, with work socks, and I was wearing palazzo pants! We thought we were so cool, and grungy-like!!!

We explored the entire area, inspected everything thoroughly despite experiencing the discomfort from blisters caused by our new shoes. Navigating the big city resulted in even more blisters, nevertheless, we found it worthwhile! We thoroughly enjoyed ourselves! It was August, before I started my second year of junior high school.

On the weekends, Jenny and I always hung out, and this time she was sleeping over. We did what typical teenagers did. We watched MTV, drank Pepsi, and ate ketchup chips. *They were my favourite.*

Jenny asked, "Want to go to Jimmy's party tonight?"

I responded with, "Sure, I'll go ask."

She had said, "It's not a typical party, this one is a hook-up party."

Jenny told me to go shave my legs saying, "cause guys didn't like picky legs when they're making out with girls."

So, I did, I shaved my legs, I went upstairs to grab a big bowl. Mom asked what I was doing. I said I needed a bowl for our chips, "OK have fun!" she called out.

As I recall the memory of it, I had felt scared and excited!

I asked Jenny, "OK, how are we going to get there?"

We thought about it for a bit, and then I said," Let's take our bikes."

I went and opened the garage so they wouldn't hear us sneak out.

We were getting ready when Jenny asked, "Is there any booze we could snatch?"

I spoke, "Yeah, I think so, there are a few bottles in the crawl space." We got on our bikes and rode to the party with a sixty-ounce bottle of alcohol in my book bag.

When we got there, we walked right in and there were a bunch people who looked trashy, smoking cigarettes, and hashing off the elements on the stove with hot knives. I wasn't sure what else, but it didn't look good.

In my head, I am thinking to myself, what am I doing here? But then I remembered what Jenny had said, "It's cool -so it must be!'

I sat on the couch, scoped out the place, and then pulled the bottle of rye out of my bag. that seemed to have brought everyone over to say hi. Jenny proceeded upstairs and disappear to visit the guy she liked.

I remained in the living room and inquired if there was anything available to mix with the bottle of Rye I brought. They replied, "There is only this one can of Coke Classic."

I responded, "Very well, mix me a drink." I then took my first sip, it was nasty, I almost puked!

So, I kept drinking and noticed everyone else was too. I was very drunk, having never had alcohol before. I looked for Jimmy. They said he was waiting downstairs. It seemed shady to me, but I went anyway. He's listening to some AC/DC songs. Pretty sure it was TNT. We were hanging out, sipping straight rye. I thought I looked cool in my Doc Martens. Suddenly, he started kissing me, and we made out, I enjoyed it. We took off my docs and my flower jumper. He had a hard-on, and I was so into this.

He asked," Do you wanna?" I said, "I think so."

He pulled out a condom and put it on, we were doing it. I was out of it. I should have gone home before that.

My cousin was nowhere to be seen, I didn't have a clue where she was either, and I, well I mean at this point, I was so drunk that I couldn't walk. Jimmy carried me up the stairs, and then some other guy had his way with me… I did not consent to this, but at this point, I was too drunk to stop it. He left, another guy came in and did the same. I vaguely remembered what happened. What I do remember was that after all those terrifying events was that I was crawling on my hands and knees, trying to get to the bathroom.

In the background I heard a woman screaming, "Get your whores out of my house!"

Someone dragged me downstairs and outside onto the sidewalk. Then, this chick, who was Jimmy's supposed girlfriend, said, "I'm going to kick your slutty ass."

At this point, from the fresh air, I was aware of what had happened and what was going on! I said, "Go right ahead, I won't feel a thing." She didn't.

Finally, my cousin showed up, helped to me on my bike, and we biked home before my dad woke up for work. I was a fucking mess and unbelievably sore. I went to sleep and passed out.

The next day, I was still sore and hungover. I went over to my cousins to hang out and for some reason she was a complete bitch to me. I remember asking her what her problem was, she flat out told me that I was a slut. I was so upset.

I said, "Yeah, things were nuts, and I honestly didn't mean to do what I did, but I was drunk, and you were supposed to be looking out for me."

"I was upstairs with Jimmy's brother trying to give him coffee to wake him up so we could mess around." Jenny had said.

After that, I was so upset with her. Yes, I was the one that did all that, but I counted on her. I had no idea that I was going to be raped.

A few months went by, and she had a new boyfriend, so I went over and hung out with her. Her boyfriend had been in jail. Jenny's cousin Chris from the other side of her family was there as well, he had no relation to me. He knew what had happened at that party, he was sixteen and I thought he was thinking that I'd sleep with him. I thought he was cute, and I'd thought I would have liked to have a boyfriend like Jenny had. Chris and I started hanging out, and for months we fooled around.

I would visit his house on weekends, but without a driver's license, I could only walk across town. Jenny only lived 3 doors down, which was convenient. We'd all hang out, drink, and do things that couples did.

It was almost a year before I finally give in to him. We slept together, drank, and messed around a lot. I was over all of the time, and I thought I loved him. I finally get the courage to tell him. He says Danke Schoen" which means thanks in German. He didn't say "I love you back."

This should have been my initial indication.

I should have taken the hint and moved on. Subsequently, he informed Jenny that I was bothersome, and he did not want me around. Jenny repeatedly conveyed this information to me, but I did not take her advice and continued to visit and engage in sexual activities with him. Chris then told me straight out that he had entered a new relationship and had moved on. Suddenly, people at school stopped wanting me around because I spent all my time with Chris. I felt hurt and sad, and I couldn't reconnect with my school friends because they said I had ditched them.

CHAPTER

My parents were building their dream home in a beautiful area in another town. They worked hard and asked if I wanted to change schools and attend a country high school for my next grade. I said sure, I still had some friends in town, but I had no problem making new ones. "OK," I had said.

At that point in my life, I was so hung up on Chris and what he had said, I was depressed.

One night, I decided to masturbate, but I was using an object that wasn't meant for that. I was so sad and upset I ended up falling asleep with the object inside of me. I was in major pain and did not realize that I had left it inside of me. I was so embarrassed that I didn't tell a soul, not my Aunt Sandy, and not even my cousin Jenny! *I thought she'd be upset*. I handled it by crying often and pretending everything was fine. I would curl up on the couch in a fetal position, despite constant pelvic throbbing.

My mom brought me to the hospital and to many doctors' appointments. I refrained from informing my doctor due my overwhelming feelings of shame. I was concerned that if anyone heard about it, it would become widely known. Despite feeling like I could die, I hid my pain for two years. I had a toxic infection, left school midway daily, and suffered from constant lower abdomen pain. At home, I'd cry alone, hoping for help.

I finally went to my family doctor. The doctor did a Pap test on me, and when she started putting the cervical clamps in, all this fluid came pouring out of me. I started crying, uncontrollably. She asked what it was, but I remained silent. I felt relieved that my two years of suffering were finally over without needing to explain. My primary care physician promptly contacted a local Urologist and arranged for me to see him immediately.

As I prepared for the appointment, I hoped that my period of silent suffering was coming to an end. During the consultation at the doctor's office, I refrained from speaking to avoid being overheard or recognized. My mother accompanied me, but I remained unaware of what to expect. We discussed undergoing a series of diagnostic tests. The doctor referred me to the hospital for further evaluation, including ultrasounds, ink dye tests, and a laparoscopy. The first two tests didn't show anything because my scar tissue had healed around the foreign object. The laparoscopy, however, revealed there was an object inside me.

My parents had previously booked a trip before all this transpired and went on a cruise ship to the Bahamas. While they were away, I was admitted to the hospital for surgery. I was nervous but had a sense of relief that it was finally going to be removed. It was expected to be a straightforward day surgery, with patients being in and out on the same day. However, in this case it proved to be more complex.

The surgery commenced with anesthesia, and there were five doctors involved in the procedure. The operation took significantly longer than anticipated, lasting six hours. The doctors encountered unexpected complexities during the surgery. Nine hours later, I woke up and found myself hooked up to every tube imaginable, including a catheter for the blood. I was all bandaged up. From my lower abdomen to my belly button, it had a row of staples. But I was on the mend with the biggest mistake that I thought had ruined my life!

My parents called my Nanny from the cruise ship to see how the procedure had gone. They were shocked but couldn't come home since they were out at sea.

I spent eleven days in the hospital, healing and receiving visits from Nanny, Grandpa, Aunt Sandy, Jenny, Will, Chris's parents, and others, all before my parents returned.

On day ten, mom and dad arrived immediately without going home first. They were happy to see me but also sad about my condition.

Dad left the room to compose himself. Mom asked, "What did you do to yourself now?"

I cried, expecting her to be happy I was alive, but she wasn't exactly mother of the year. I told her what I did, and she cried and felt terrible that I hadn't wanted to turn to her for help.

On day eleven, I was ready to be discharged. My mom and Aunt Sandy were at the hospital, and they made me laugh. Aunt Sandy was the best, I was in so much pain, and I was not supposed to laugh, because my muscles were all cut. I placed a pillow over them so I could press down if I had to. I still remember them trying to make jokes. Making me smile!

I was home and had a nurse who would come daily to the house and cleaned my incision and bandaged me back up. She was great.

I asked her if I could pull my own staples out, and she said, "Yes, of course!"

My invasive surgery was so severe that I had to take off school for about eight weeks. I had to heal not just physically but mentally from everything that had happened, especially what I had put myself through. To this day, I think I should have spoken to a specialist, psychologist, or someone. I was offered to, but I can't remember.

All that I know was that I was ready to take on the world!

CHAPTER

When I was eighteen years old, I went to my eye specialist. He told my parents I could finally have the cataract surgery that I had been born with, removed by laser surgery. I finally had clear vision for the first time in my life. I was seeing bright colors Wow, Amazing!

I'm graduating high school, should have a semester ago. I lost a lot of time with the surgery. But I was healed, I had a few scars but good to go!

I had a new boyfriend, Kev. He was so good to me; I told him all about what had happened to me. He was truly ok with everything. He was the best, and we were always together!

We were going to prom; my mom had bought me a beautiful dress that fit me like a glove. I wasn't worried about my scar, I knew it gave me strength and helped me realize what I went through.

I am incredibly strong!

Prom was beautiful, I had graduated! My future at this point was looking amazing, with Kev, we both had jobs, and we had planned a future together.

Finally, we had moved out of our parent's house and moved into an apartment above my grandparents' place. I loved it there; I was so close to them. Every morning before work I'd stopped in and had coffee and listened to all the family gossip. Kev and I were doing so well; I had two part-time jobs, and Kev worked at a new factory in town.

One day, I came home from work, and he proposed to me! I was so happy and so of course I had said yes! We were always doing everything together; he was my lover and also my best friend. I called my mom and dad; they were ecstatic for us. We are both twenty-one now and we decided that we should start saving money for a down payment on a house.

As the year goes by, we start arguing and we were getting stressed about money and we realized that we couldn't put money aside for a down payment on a house. We ended up moving back home, I ended up getting a much better job and was able to save. We were ready to buy our house. It was perfect, we put an offer for one and got it. It was ours, and we both worked so hard to obtain it.

We were engaged, we had a new house, both had our own vehicles, and I was feeling on top of the world. We finally started planning for our wedding. In exactly one year from our engagement, we were married!

I was married at twenty-five years old, back then, I had talked about the possibility of having children. It had been almost seven years since my major surgery. I was unsure how it would go.

I had a doctor's appointment with a gynecologist to see about having children. He was the same doctor who saved me during my initial surgery. He told me I had to go for some tests because I had too much scar tissue, and that my fallopian tubes were all twisted. I was honestly heartbroken but still remained optimistic. I loved kids. I always wanted to have children.

I went home and called my mom on the phone; she cried and said, "Now I won't have grandkids." I cried and told her she was fucking selfish.

Now, I have to prepare for another surgery to remove scar tissue so the doctor can determine if I can have children. My spouse and I were facing this together in our first home. I finally had a man who loved me and would take care of me! Months had gone by, everything was great.

So, I thought…

CHAPTER

Kev was into outdoor sports and he wanted to buy a four-wheeler, so we remortgaged the house and used the little bit of equity to pay for the recreational vehicle. We had gone out with them all the time, especially in the winter, I didn't like it. I had been frozen the whole time because I had not been outfitted properly for the weather. Kev would go out all the time with his buddies too and drop me off at my parents on the way out. I was okay with it, until I wasn't.

It was wintertime, I was scheduled to go in for my laparoscopy, day surgery, to remove the scar tissue from the previous surgery. I am supposed to be out the same day; I was in the hospital for six days. Kev's mom had come to see me almost every day and my family. Kev was working night shift eleven pm to seven am. He could have popped in on his way to work, he hadn't. Kev had not visited, not once. That had hurt me so much. I honestly thought he knew of the emotional support that I needed. That conduct showed me exactly who he was.

I had been discharged a day early, my surgery consisted of a similar incision just horizontal in the same lower abdomen areas similar to a cesarean. I had been in large amount of pain and was given morphine for it. I had given my husband a phone call because I was so excited to go home. Kev responded by stating that he was not excited to have me back home because it was snowing out and it was a beautiful night for four-wheeling. His tone was pouty on the phone, he had claimed that I wasn't supposed to be home a day early. My husband did come get me, but I was so hurt, I was feeling that he'd rather hang out with the guys than me!

On the way home in the car, I could barely move. The doctor told me not to walk up and down stairs or lift anything over ten pounds.

We had gotten into the house and he was acting like a child because I would not let him go play with his friends! Your wife had just had major surgery, and you want to hang out with the guys?!

I walked up the stairs, *our bedroom was in the attic*, grabbed my own blanket, and pillow, then went back downstairs and got on the couch with no help from him. Back then, I can still remember how absolutely pissed I was. I had told him to go if that's what would make him happy, and he did!

I was home by myself, and my wheels were turning, I wanted out of this relationship. I wanted to leave this little boy who hadn't grown up yet! I was off work for about six weeks, and I planned a drastic change.

CHAPTER

I had been working a night shift job, and an older guy was giving me some much-needed attention. This guy wasn't anyone special I was interested in at the time, just someone to talk to-receive attention, someone to pass the time, that's all.

We started sneaking for coffee back then before our shift. That wasn't ok, I was still married at the time. But at this point, I didn't care anymore. I knew drastic action was necessary to end our short marriage. I couldn't live my life always being second.

Kev's dad would go fishing and hunting up north, leaving his mom at home. My parents did everything together—darts, golf, you name it!

One day, I went to my coworker's house, and we kissed. I was nervous and knew it was wrong, but it's fine for me, because in my mind the relationship was already over with Kev. I'm getting all this attention, it's great, Kev and I were like roommates, no sex, and no communication.

One night, Kev had gone to sleep at the cottage, and I was home alone so I decided to go out to have a drink with my girlfriend Chantal, she was at my wedding party. We are having some drinks, and I told my coworker to meet us there, and he had. My husband Kev comes back from the cottage and catches us together!

So, my marriage to Kev was over and it was about a year after the surgery. It's surreal that we gave up so quickly after only two years of marriage, despite being together for seven years.

I went through major depression. It was awful, and everything fell apart because we both gave up too easily. We had sold the house and divided everything up, right down to the items of the knives and forks.

I had moved back to my parents' home; I was currently experiencing a period of transition. My father was very understanding and reassured me that I would regain stability and happiness in due time, as there were many opportunities ahead for me.

Conversely, my mother expressed her disappointment by stating that I had jeopardized my future, emphasizing that I once had everything. In response, I conveyed to her that personal happiness is the most important thing of all, and without it, other achievements lose their significance.

CHAPTER

I was legally divorced.

I was back hanging out with my cousin Jenny. Her now husband, Will, together they have two small kids. My Friends from work, were dating, partying, and having a great time. I was about to be twenty-seven years old. I was working at a fast-food restaurant making little money and living life like a renewed teenager.

I met a man named Ben, who was slightly younger than me. We had some things in common and ended up moving in together. His entire family lived in a large old house that they were renovating with the intent of selling. The rent was affordable, and we resided in a refurbished attic apartment.

His aunt at the time didn't like me, she thought I was obsessed with him. I wasn't obsessed; I simply appreciated his attention. I had a difficult upbringing, and my ex-husband and I had separated. Yes, I was going through a hard time, but I was not obsessed.

Our relationship was brief. I moved in with a coworker who was incredible, and we often socialized together and went to parties. At that time, I was twenty-eight years old.

My father's workplace was closing permanently, and my parents are moving seven hours away. They wanted me to move into my own apartment to ensure I can manage independently if anything would happen.

As an only child, I had been accustomed to material possessions rather than emotional affection. I had decided that it's time to love myself and be self-sufficient because I've felt that I been "*left*" my whole life.

My parents helped me find an affordable apartment, providing most of their furniture as well as a phone and cable. I had a car bill. Managing everything on my own was challenging, but I made it work despite having no prior experience living independently.

My parents were selling their house. My father was currently residing in Michigan, commuting between home and work, which was difficult for them both.

While I was working on one occasion, my mom stopped in and told me dad had a heart attack. She was frantic and had to drive up there by herself. Before she left me at work, she had told me that everything would be ok. I was glad that my dad was ok, and I was thanking God!

It had seemed that he had a minor heart attack, he had just been stressed to the max working at this new plant and working way too much. It was too many hours away from us. My parents house offer was accepted, and they found a lovely home down south, seven hours away. They hoped to move back in about four years they tell me. My dad was fifty-four years old; mom was fifty years old at the time. They only had a few years to go for their full retirement pension. They packed up and went on their way to their new home, we said our goodbyes.

CHAPTER

I was twenty-nine years old living my life, hanging out with friends doing what a single woman at that age did. I had no worries in sight and my dad was on the mend, and the distance between my mom and I was good, her not around to bring me down.

I lived near a shabby bar. My cousin and her husband visited for drinks and suggested karaoke there, I agreed but said I wouldn't sing. We walked over, and they reminisced about the past, which I didn't remember as fondly, so I just laughed and ignored them. *As I recall, it was the major reason why I've had all the traumatic issues that I will have to live with forever.* Anyway, we had a lot of fun; we danced and carried on back then.

I recall there was this older guy who was smiling and flirting with me from the dance floor; his name was Rob. He had bought me a drink and initiated a conversation. At this point, I found him to be quite confident and amusing. I provided him with my phone number and later discovered that he was almost ten years older than me and had two daughters in their early teens. Despite these differences, I accept the situation.

I returned to spend time with my cousins and shared the details with them. We all enjoyed ourselves, and then I went back to my apartment alone.

A few days later, Rob contacted me and had invited me to his house. I am excited about finally going on a date with someone who has their life in order, and I am trying to do the same. I go over, I had brought pj's, beer, toothbrush, you know all the necessities. We listened to music and talked, we learned a lot about each other. I was drinking wine, and I was very drunk. I had a really good feeling about this guy! I felt like I'm in LA LA land.

The next morning, I was hung over and I had to work at six am. *Not good at all for me, ha-ha but it was fine, I'm a big girl, been through worse!* On my break who stopped in, Rob, I wasn't expecting that! I was all smiles; he was as well!

A week had passed, and Rob started asking me questions that related to the movie, "*HITCH.*" He had asked various questions about the film while we were enjoying wine together. We ended up spending the night together. At this point, I was still renting my apartment, although I was rarely there. He introduced me to his daughters, who were eager to meet me. I remember feeling nervous, as I had never dated anyone with children before. Considering I can't have any kids, I'm not sure about that aspect in this fresh relationship. Everything about this relationship had felt new and exciting! Robs girls stay with their mom every other week. When I was there, it's just a bit of an adjustment to get used to. I was meeting Rob's friends, who parties on weekends, playing poker, and hanging out at the bar where I met Rob. The women were great and had welcomed me warmly.

I had never been happier.

We went on shopping trips and vacations. One day his friends had asked if we wanted to go on a trip. I couldn't afford a trip with the couple and had asked my parents for money so I could go with Rob. They refused. I was upset but got over it.

He was leaving in two weeks with all his friends to go south and I was over every single night. We were having mad crazy sex. It was so much fun, his daughters were there, and he was acting like they weren't. I remember feeling that was weird.

He had left for the trip, and I was back at my shitty apartment doing my own thing, working, and chilling. I was visiting my Aunt Sandy, going over for suppers. I'm telling her about Rob, she was so happy for me, *I thought back then that this could be the one to change my life. I could have it all, love, respect, and trust. You know everything you hope for in a relationship!*

I hadn't told mom and dad just yet about Rob. I had wanted to wait a little while longer. In the meantime, I was hanging out with my friends and cousins, working, and keeping busy.

I'm at my Aunt Sandy's hanging out one night, and Rob calls me on my cell phone. I was so excited that he had called me from his trip. He just called to say that he missed me, and he couldn't wait to see me. Only three days till he was home! I had let him go on the phone, and I was excited and happy that he was thinking of me; I told my aunt everything. My heart was pounding, I could barely stop smiling.

I remember that he had to see his girls first before he could come and see me, and I was getting used to being the girlfriend of almost two teenagers. I was trying my best to care and help out. I am not used to sharing anything. I was an only child. I do my best to wait patiently. *Haha!*

Everything was back to normal; I was on cloud nine. Everything was perfect with new friends', a new life. My past was in the past.

CHAPTER

It had been my father's birthday weekend, and I finally decided that I wanted to introduce my parents to Rob. We had been together for about five months, and he had kindly taken me to visit my parents in Michigan. It was my first time there, and his gesture of taking me was very considerate. We had a wonderful time, and it was great to see them after six months. Due to the long distance, I hadn't called much.

For some reason though, I had this feeling that I owed Rob.

He realized that my pay checks weren't keeping up with his lifestyle, so he suggested that I change my job. All his friends' wives were waitresses, and they were making a killing. So, I had quit my fast-food job like he suggested. I thought I would excel because of my great personality with customers. I also rented out my apartment to this guy I knew from the restaurant, Matt. I figured I was never there, so why not?

I had struggled with stress at that job, especially during supper rush. I did try my best and did enjoy collaborating with my colleagues, but they excelled while I was just trying to keep up. Still, bringing home tips each night was better than minimum wage. My performance wasn't satisfactory, but I was still new at that position but eventually I started to find my rhythm. I kept taking shifts and doing my best to match the pace of those people at my work who had ten years of experience.

In August, the gang had decided to book a trip to NYC. They had asked me to attend! *I was so stoked!* I had never really been anywhere.

I asked Rob if I could go, he said, "Of course, but do you have your own money?"

"Yes," I had said, "not much, but some."

I jumped in **Nat's** car, with the girls, Alex, Lisa, and Nat! Nat was and is the best! I remember her telling me not to worry about anything! Everything was going to be amazing! While we were there, we shopped, went to restaurants, and walked everywhere! It was so much fun!

On the last day of our trip, we were in New Jersey at a mall. We were standing at a sandwich shop line up at the food court. We ordered our food, two Philly steak and cheese subs and Snapple Iced teas.

We walked to our table, and Rob showed me the new shoes he had bought. Jokingly, I said, "Only losers wear those types of shoes."

Rob lost his temper, poured his iced tea on my lunch, and said, "Who's the loser now?"

I walked away with tears in my eyes, feeling trapped and embarrassed among his friends. Only afterwards Nat spoke to me, expressing disbelief at his actions and reassured me that he sometimes reacts like that because he's sensitive about his style. I promised not to tease him again.

I stayed at my apartment with my roommate, and I didn't forget what had happened in Jersey. I was back with Rob and the kids, hanging out, doing our thing, all was great.

He had mentioned in passing, "Hey, you might as well get rid of your apartment."

I responded with, "Really? Are you serious?" while we were having drinks.

I was so happy, I remember thinking I finally had it all, I was making pretty good money at the time, and in a good relationship. Everything was amazing!

I had called Matt who was renting my place the next day and let him know that he could have the place permanently. I sold all my furniture because Rob had no room for it! Matt had taken my furniture, it had felt like it was meant to be.

I moved all my clothes into Rob's house and small stuff I wanted to keep at this point, and he was buying a new house. The house had needed major renovations done. Rob was stressed to the max and was being a real douche bag toward me because he couldn't really afford the place.

That's when things had changed quickly, Rob argued with me and said that I didn't have any money. We were fighting and yelling all the time. I remember that I let it slide because I knew that he wasn't himself.

When I was by myself, I cried and kept it to myself. I didn't want people to know what was going on.

***

It was my thirtieth Birthday! There was about twenty people out for supper, celebrating. Once dinner was over, everyone had gone back to the house to celebrate. My parents had also called me to wish me a happy birthday. I remember feeling very happy! I had spoken to my dad; he had told me that he was so proud of me, as always. While at the party Rob told me that he used my birthday as an excuse to have all of *his friends over to check out his new pad.* I responded by crying and went to bed, while everyone was still there.

I had come to the realization that he was selfish and a show-off. At this point I had witnessed so many red flags. But I continued to just swept it all under the carpet.   It was just more of the same thing I had seen all my life.

My mom and dad would argue all the time, and Mom would often yell at me all the time. So, to me I thought it could be worse, I could be alone, and I couldn't stand being alone.

***

It was now the Christmas holiday season. My mom and dad were home for the holidays. They are staying at Aunt Sandy and Uncle Bob's. I am visiting lot. I missed them, I haven't seen them in months. Mom and dad were visiting everyone as much as they could.

Dad hadn't seemed himself I remember. Aunt Sandy had one of her party's, we always had such a blast. Rob had showed up. We listened to old music, including American Pie by Don McLean. That was my dad's favorite song! I remember it being such a fun time! The next day it was Christmas Eve.

On my way to the grocery store, I had seen my dad walking down a main street in town. It was unusual, and I sensed something was up. That evening, we went to my Nanny's as usual for drinks, appetizers, and good company. I didn't mention to my dad about seeing him earlier that day.

The next day we had been very busy, we had Christmas supper at Rob's house and my parents had popped in. Then they left the next day to go back to Michigan.

Rob and I were invited to his friend's New Year's Eve party. We would be attending, socializing, and participating in various activities.

But at this point, he just uses me for his pleasure. Basically, only sex. He belittles and degrades me in front of his friends' by telling everyone he bought a sex toy, because I'm horrible at the only thing that, I'm good at.. Now I'm outraged and want to leave.. but I had nowhere to go and so I end up going home with Rob.

I had struggled with waitressing, but I had continued to persevere because it was the only way I was able to earn a reasonable income. I remember I maintained a positive attitude while working and tried to conceal my true feelings. I only expressed my true emotions when I was under the influence of alcohol.

CHAPTER

Rob and I had plans to go to Sexapalooza.

This was a consumer experience, shopping, shows all about -"the experience." It appeared to me that it was a very big deal for Rob! We were going with another couple Lori and Steve they also were all about that lifestyle, and I had also heard that they were swingers. I had often found myself talking about being interested in sexual topics to gain their acceptance, even though I had been told that I wasn't successful in any other area.

We had been scheduled to leave around three o'clock that afternoon, and the place was an hour away. I had gone to the mall to buy something to wear. That night, I had felt a little bit of anxiety just wondering what was going to happen at the event we were about to attend. As I was about to arrive at the mall, and I had gotten a call from Rob, he said that I needed to come home, so I had asked why? He had a sense of urgency in his voice. I asked what's wrong. He had said that I needed to come home now because he had bought flowers for me. I was surprised since he never bought me anything before. I then turn around, and drove back home, feeling excited. When I had walked through the door, *this is the worst,* Rob tells me my Aunt Sandy had called him and informed him that my dad had passed away. My mom had found my dad in the drive-way. My dad was only fifty-five years old!

I remember that I started yelling and screaming, "*NO, NO!*" I pushed Rob into to a wall, saying, "No this isn't true, you're lying. Why would you say something like this."

I'm losing my shit. Rob tells me that we'll have to get ready because your aunt and uncle are on their way to pick us up, and we were going to Michigan. I was just exhausted and numb at this point, I was in disbelief!

My aunt and uncle pulled up in the driveway, I was all packed. Aunt Sandy came running up to me, she was crying and consoling me. I remember it being a very quiet drive to Michigan, I had smoked a lot and sipped on some coffee. It was so smokey in the car because we were all smoking. I couldn't even see outside. *Yuck!* I had cried all the way to my parent's place! The drive was horrible, roads were full of snow. We arrived at my parents' house around ten pm that night. When I walked into their house, that I had only been in one time prior to this, I had felt like I couldn't breathe, I felt like I was going to hyperventilate. It just didn't feel real; it was all just a blur.

Seeing my mom broken, it was hard to take because I'd never seen her like this before. It was strange, when I had walked in, I didn't know anyone at their house, there were people there that I had never met! We had all just sat there and had drinks, trying to numb the pain. Crying so much was the only thing I could do from losing my dad. My dad was such a comedian. He was always making jokes, that was a nice memory that I remember of him.

The next day we had awoken to plan the wake and funeral parlor. I had picked out an urn, and I remember thinking, *'wow, I didn't think I'd ever be doing this with my mom.'* But these are the times, I had to be strong and carry on. It was such a long day, and my mom was so strong. My aunt and I were there to support her. Rob and my uncle had stayed at home' while we did all the running around.

The next day was his wake and funeral and there were all these people at mom's house, sending food and flowers. My dad's best friend from home, Nik, had flown in too, it was unbelievable! I remember feeling that it was really nice to see him again!

It was a beautiful service; it was very nice of Rob to do the eulogy, considering he had only met him a few times. That night it was so busy, mom and dad's friends were at the house, cheering for my dad's life, singing American pie in remembrance. It was hard to believe that this would be the first time he wasn't there, to sing along with us!

That night Rob told me in bed that the only reason he came to my dad's funeral was because it looked good in front of the others. Not for moral support.

I couldn't believe what I had heard! I cried and I yelled and said, "Are you fucking kidding me??? I just lost my father, and you tell me this on the night of his funeral??? Go fuck yourself!" I cried all night and was in a fetal position.

The next day, when we were going back home, I was completely numb. I had lost my dad, and I knew my boyfriend was a piece of shit!

I just remember feeling *stuck!*

I had nowhere to go, and I needed to go home and figure out what to do, I could barely make ends meet.

My mom was just heartbroken and had to deal with all this on her own because she is seven hours away from me. I had needed to work. I had no choice but to stay with Rob. I couldn't afford an apartment or anything else.

So, I stayed and put up with everything! I was an absolute mess, a few months go by, and I was still numb, as if this life was not real. Mom and dad had only come home every holiday weekend, so my mom was just coming home to visit on the next holiday.

CHAPTER

Rob was having a big poker party with all his friends. His kids were there, hanging out in their room. We were all drinking listening to music, they were playing cards, and I was just hanging out. It was a lot of fun. I kept going over to Rob asking him questions, not entirely sure what I was asking him. But I knew I had annoyed him; he was getting ruder and more ignorant. He was a tough guy around his friends.

At the end of the night, I got all depressed and started thinking of my dad and being pushed away by Rob. I remember feeling that I wanted to die. He didn't want me; and my mom was seven hours away. There was just so much going on in my head, especially after I had been drinking a lot that night, it was amplifying everything. I went into the bathroom and took out some Percocet out of the medicine cabinet. I intended to just take a few to numb the pain, but I'm not too sure how many I took. I just knew that I didn't want to be here anymore.

He came into the bathroom after a while, he was yelling and screaming at me telling me I just wanted attention.

I said, "No, I just want to be with my dad!"

He called the ambulance, he was absolutely pissed at me for what I had done, and his girls were there during all of that.

I went to the hospital; they pumped my stomach. I was ok, but I was depressed, embarrassed, and everything all in one! A doctor came in and prescribed me some antidepressants and a psychiatrist. I ended up staying overnight at the hospital and I remember I called Rob so many times, but he didn't answer, nor did he seem to care.

He had called my mom to tell her what happened, and my mom was upset. I ended up staying at my Aunt Sandy's house for a few weeks. I was talking to Rob here and there. Hoping that we would get back together, I was addicted to him, even though we were like oil and water.

***

Mom had finally come home to visit for Easter. She was staying at Aunt Sandy's for a week, to get everything in order. Mom had decided to put the house up for sale and sell dad's jeep. It had been three months since dad had passed.

I needed to bring my car in for an oil change, that day. I drove an alright car; it just needed some repairs, but I didn't have any money to fix it. Mom and Aunt Sandy were drinking early that afternoon, they were drinking wine beer, whatever was available. They were having a good time listening to Patsy Cline. I came over and said that I was bringing my car in for an oil change, and they decided to jump in.

We walked in to the shop and my aunt is hooting and hollering. She was embarrassing but hilarious! My mom was pretty drunk since they had both been drinking red wine all afternoon.

Ooh boy, I had a Pepsi!

I was so embarrassed because everyone at the shop was staring at us.

The mechanics looked at my car, and my mom told them to give her a quote for all the work. The total came up to three thousand dollars. While I was waiting, I was walking around the lot and spotted this super cute two-door hatchback, and I was in love!

Mom spotted it too, she asks how much, and they tell her the price. My mom tells the mechanic to leave my car on the hoist. My uncle had come to the shop just then and picked us all up at the dealership. We went back to their house. The dealership had my mom's number when they were ready to let her know about the car. My uncle had an old SUV in the driveway that had been off the road for a few years.

It needed a ton of work. He had offered it to me for ten thousand dollars. I told him, "No, sorry, I'd like the new one, it's only a year-old little hatchback that had barely any kilometers on it, and it was perfect for me."

We called the car salesman back and accepted the deal for the new vehicle; I remember feeling so happy! *My Uncle, however, was not!* I did think, and still do, that this was a debt-free ticket for him! So, when I declined his offer, he wasn't happy at all.

I left and went to pick up the car and then returned to my aunt and uncle's. By now they were pretty drunk, and my uncle was angry! He started calling me a spoiled brat, and that I had everything handed to me on a silver platter. My mom lost it on him! He then took a can of beer and slammed it on the counter; it sprayed everywhere; and then he took the pizza box and pitched it across the basement.

My mom cornered him and said, "Don't you *EVER* talk to My daughter like that again! Let's get the fuck out of here. Let's go to Nannys." I agreed and offered to drive.

My mom didn't accept, instead she drove her SUV. I wasn't happy, but she was already pulling out of the driveway so there was no chance of changing her mind. I said "I'll meet you at Nanny's;" she promised she would!

I showed up at Nanny's about ten minutes later; she was shocked to see me. It was eleven-thirty pm at night. Mom hadn't gotten there yet. Nanny and I called her cell phone twenty times, but there was no answer.

I fell asleep waiting for her, I had thought about going back to Aunt Sandy's. The phone rang later that morning, it was the police, mom had been picked up for drinking and driving. The police officer explained what happened to me over the phone and I could pick her up after two am. I was so relieved she was ok, but my mom was so upset that she was trying to drive back home to Michigan.

I had driven to the police station; mom was there crying and yelling at the police officer! She was so emotionally exhausted, and her alcohol level was way over the limit! Thank God my mom was ok, and no one was hurt, except her pride. My mom was charged with driving under the Influence. She lost her license for a year! I brought her back to Nanny's. It was roughly four am in the morning. My mom cried with the loss of her license, she knows she lost her independence, especially since she's seven hours away from home.

In the morning, she packed up all her things. My grandparents drove my mom to pick up her car at the police station. My grandpa drove her back home to Michigan, and my mom paid for grandpa's train ticket back home. My Aunt Sandy went to stay with her for the next few months. My dad has been passed for three months, and now she has lost her license, stuck in Michigan, away from her entire family. I, on the other hand, had made up with Rob. I also didn't want to be at Aunt Sandy's; I couldn't believe how everything had gone down. I lost respect for my uncle; I decided that he was the reason this happened! I mean, my mom should not have driven, but if it weren't for him losing his shit, that might not have happened!

I was back working at the restaurant, a few months went by, and everything is back to routine. Father's Day is approaching; I was to meet with my manager, Carol. I was so nervous, and I knew that I sucked at waitressing. Carol told me that Stephanie is leaving and there was a full-time position coming up for me. I was so excited! Rob was having another party; I could not wait to tell everyone! My new friend Nat was there; she's happy for me! We were all having a great time at the party for the first time in months! Everyone leaves, we cleaned everything up and I remember that I was smiling from ear to ear!

CHAPTER

Rob and I woke up late from cleaning up the mess from the night before. The phone rang: it was my manager, Carol, who tells me she was letting me go. I honestly couldn't believe that she was telling me this!

I had proceeded to give her a hard time, I said, "Are you serious, today is Father's Day, and you're letting me go on this day?"

I was crying and mortified. The conversation ended and I said, "Thank you for your time," and I hung up the phone.

I was so upset and hurt, and Rob wasn't happy either, he stated that he had felt bad for me.. *imagine that?*

Later, Nat and her husband pulled up in the driveway, I ran out of the house and told her all the bullshit. She couldn't believe it either. I said and to top it off today was the first Father's Day without my dad.

Everything was just going in a downward spiral; I had felt like I couldn't do anything right. Depression continued to kick in full force.

I started looking for another job, in the waitressing field, even though I was still terrible at it. It was the only way to make decent money I thought without having an education. I was then hired at another popular restaurant. It wasn't too bad; tips were good, and I was doing well at my job. It was nice having cash in my pocket again.

I felt like I was thriving again, I was in a better headspace!

Rob and I, our relationship seemed to be going well, mom moved to dad's friends place. He and his wife were living in another province, so they rented out their home to my mom to help her get back on her feet. My mom was planning on buying a house, setting her future up, and glad she was back in her hometown. That was very nice of my dad's friends to do that for my mom! They were amazing friends. At this point mom still had her license. Very lucky! A few months went by she found the perfect home! Not long after she moved in and had made it possible to start her life without my dad.

At this point I was still on and off with Rob. I was so infatuated with him; it was disgusting. I realize now that we were so incompatible. It seemed as if I was never good enough for him.

One evening, I was out having a girl's night, and we were all drinking wine and that had made me intoxicated early in the evening. *Well, I would drink it too fast, rather than sipping on it.* I was supposed to stay over at my friend's house, considering that Rob and I were in an argument again. He said he needed his space, which meant he was going to hook up with someone.

He surely cheated on me many times, I thought, but I had no proof, just a feeling. I was going to sleep on my friend's couch, but instead I got up while the others were sleeping. I was going to drive but took a cab instead.

I showed up at Rob's around two am. He answered the door! He wasn't happy to see me at all. At this point in our relationship, he was never really happy to see me. I had enjoyed randomly popping in to check on him! He let me in, then we argued for a bit, had angry sex, as usual, finished then argued some more! He told me to leave, I wouldn't, he tells me that he just used me, as for sex! At this point I am crying, yelling, and screaming. He threw me up to the wall and said you need to leave now and threatened to call the police!

I couldn't believe it, I was emotionally wrecked, physically, he had laid his hands on me and was now stating he was going to calling the police, I got the fuck out of there!

I walked to my friend's house about twenty minutes on foot. She answered the door and was in shock at the looks of me! We sat outside in the backyard on her front porch, early in the morning.

She brewed a pot of coffee. We sipped on it while I told her the entire emotional experience that had happened to me. She was good friends with Rob and was in shock that he could be that abusive to me! After I was done explaining the details, I left and went home to clean up and rest.

At that moment I had started to finally realize that being with him was terrible for my mental health. No one really thought about that, back then. The next day another friend of mine wanted to hear about what happened, she was genuinely concerned for me. At the end of the conversation, she made me promise to never, and I mean never, hook up with him again! She gave me an ultimatum, she said firmly, our friendship, or him. At that point it was hard to choose because of my addiction to him, but I chose friendship!

CHAPTER

Everyone was extremely happy, especially my mother, that I had separated from Rob. My mom was still trying to pick up the pieces of her own life. I lived with her because I could not afford to live in apartment on my own just yet. I was working part time at a superstore. I had barely any education, just high school, and I was divorced with no money, and no extra income.

My mom was amazing that she let me stay with her rent free. I was able to still live a great life, I was dating guys and could afford to go out with my friends. It was almost a year since Rob broke up and I had moved on. In early spring, I had decided to make an online dating profile. I was on it for a few months, and I went out for supper with guys, here and there. Nothing to special. I wasn't feeling it.

It was mid-summer, and I met this guy named Chuck, and we started dating. He was so good looking; he had money, a boat, and worked for the government. I travelled back and forth to see him on his boat. We would have suppers quite often, and we enjoyed each other's company.

On this particular weekend, I was invited to a party. I was asked to bring steaks for the two of us. I was thrilled to meet his friends, and I had so much fun. They all seemed nice and friendly, and they asked me what I did for a living. So, I told them that I was a cashier at a superstore. I wasn't ashamed, nor did I feel that I should have been.

The next day, I went home and couldn't wait to go back. I texted Chuck that evening to say goodnight and he didn't respond. I found it strange because he always texted back. I felt like he was glued to his phone or sitting on it and now he was ghosting me.. I felt upset and was obsessed with getting some sort of response, so I started calling him. He finally answered and apologized to me, and used his daughter as an excuse as to why he didn't pick up the phone at first.

He finally decided to be honest with me and said, "Sorry, I don't think your right for me." After hanging out for over a month.

I asked him, WHY? He explains it again saying, "Well, you live far and well you only work part time as a cashier."

I said to him, "Well, it was all good when you read my profile. I was upfront and honest. It seems like everything changed after I met your friends."

And that was the end of that.

'Why they didn't like me?' I thought.. whatever.. that's horrible to be judgmental towards me.. especially we had sex plenty of times beforehand. I was good enough for that though, eh?...Fuck you!

***

I was home all the time after that and all my girlfriends are with their new boyfriends. I was just working and hanging out with Aunt Sandy, mom, and the girls every now and then. I was still having a great time! No stress and no worries. It was the beginning of August, and I decided I wanted to better myself by taking college courses. I figured ...maybe I could do more. There was a college about an hour away offering dietary aide courses. I remember feeling very excited to learn and feel better about myself! I decided to enrolled in the course, so did Nat!

I was so pumped, and I could see my future was changing; I had decided that I was in charge of my happiness!

I was at home and so delighted to tell my mom about my plan. I told her, and she couldn't believe it! She was happy for me but skeptical and thought that I wouldn't go through with it. But I had my best friend Nat with me to have my back and help me, we would help each other.

I continued to be on a dating app and came across this handsome guy who had the nicest smile I'd ever seen. His name was Joey. I messaged him back, but he was hard to communicate with on the dating site. I gave him my number so we could text back and forth, but he wasn't really into that either. I thought to myself, well, I'm not sure how this will work out. He'd call me and I'd text him back. I went to work the next day and talked to this young girl I worked with and told her about the texting issue. She laughed and said to just answer the phone and say hi. I didn't know why but for some reason I was really shy to talk to him, and I got the feeling that he was someone special, so I had been extremely nervous!

Finally, that evening, I had answered the phone in the best 'hello,' I had ever said! He asked if I would like to go out on a date to one of the popular restaurants in town. I said yes! He said he'd pick me up. I was like wow, okay!

Joey picks me up, he was driving a Jeep, it was so nice, it was just like the one my dad had before he passed away. I came out of the house, and he was standing with a beautiful smile and waiting by the passenger side of the car to open my door for me. We are on our way to the restaurant and talking, I was nervous as hell, because I believe that this guy is something special. He just speaks differently, I felt like he has a heart, if that makes any sense. We order drinks, he orders a Guinness beer, which I've never seen or heard of, I order a glass of house red. I was a red drinker back then. We get our burgers and he's so classy I think because he eats his food with a knife and fork, but me on the other hand, I am messy! As we are eating, we're talking about life and work. I was extremely excited to tell him that I was enrolled in college and starting the following week. He is very interested and impressed because I'm now thirty-four years old and going back to school. He made me smile and it encouraged me to be even more proud of myself for taking big steps.

On the way back to my house, I was feeling a sense of relief, it was a nice time. He gets out of his jeep, opens my door, and says good night, promising to call me tomorrow.

I smiled and agreed, feeling happy inside. I thought, "What a great guy! I'm glad I went on this date."

My mom was interested in hearing all about him, she asks many questions and. was impressed by what I told her. "Are you going out with Joey again?" My mom asked. I said that I hoped so He called me on Friday to ask if I'd like to go to the fair with him. It was Labor Day weekend. I said sure calmly, while I have butterflies stirring in my tummy, I was full of excitement!

On the Saturday, I have to get all my furniture out of the storage bin after two years of paying for this crappy furniture that was worth nothing. My mom and Aunt Sandy were helping me take care of the furniture moving it to mom's and we sell some of it.

I was getting ready to go out on date number two with Joey. Mom and Aunt Sandy were so happy for me! I am driving out to the country; I've never been out this way before. I miss the turn, and I had to call Joey. He laughed and gave me the right directions to get to his house. I pulled into this gravel driveway. I look towards me, and there is this beautiful country home. It has a cute front porch, and an attached garage, it is stunning. I was so nervous walking up the stairs, praying that I wouldn't fall, or trip, I am so clumsy. Joey comes to answer the door, He opens it, says hello, and welcomes me in. I walked in and am looking around. I'm very impressed. It's beautifully decorated, considering he's a bachelor.

He says, "Are you ready? The fair is starting soon, let's go check it out."

I said, "Yes, I'm in!"

I had never been to a county fair before, we got there in five minutes. His sister, brother-in-law, niece, and nephew are at the fair as well. His niece was going to perform and sing on stage as a contestant. I thought it was an interesting way of meeting family for the first time. It was nice to meet everyone. We grabbed a beer at the beer tent and chatted with his sister. Her name was Kali, she was so sweet and offered to drive us home later.

Joey said, "No, I think we will just have one as we were here to see Mya sing."

I thought to myself, *wow, that was incredibly sweet of her to offer, what a nice gesture.*

We were under the canopy where the little stage was all set up. Mya goes up, on stage started to sing. I looked at Joey and said wow that little girl was amazing!!!! He had tears in his eyes. I smiled and kept on watching Mya! I literally was blown away by her talent.

Later after we had to drop off a trailer at his family's. He asked if I minded, I said, "No, let's go!"

We went to his parents, grabbed the trailer, then we drove out to his brothers-in-law, they owned a local farm. I had never been out this way before, it was so nice as we drove around on gravel roads with the top down on the jeep. We got to the farm, and his whole family was there. I met his dad, sister-in-law, brother-in-law, and two nephews. They offered me a beer. We stood there and talked to them. I was so nervous. We left, they all said good bye, it was so nice to meet them. I smiled, and Joey opened the jeep door for me again. He was such a sweetie.

We were headed to a country store, where I was surprised to see an LCBO. We bought beer and chips. I messaged my Aunt Sandy, excited to share how the date was going and mentioned the store. She asked where I was, but I didn't know.

We arrived at his house with our snacks and beer. We went on the back deck and started having a few drinks, listening to music, having a great time! We ordered pizza and chilled watched a movie. Fell asleep on the couch, we had cuddled up! We woke up and I realized we had slept in the same bed and woke up in each other's arms. Nothing sexual had happened. That was a great night.

It's Sunday morning, Joey asked if I would like scrambled eggs and bacon for breakfast. I replied with a yes please, smiling from ear to ear. He told me to relax and watch TV. He asked me if I needed ketchup. I put my own on the side of my plate and used the rest of it.

He gave me a look. I said, "what? I like ketchup."

He smiled. We were watching Three's Company, my all-time favorite TV show. I was in aww with everything that had taken place.

When the date was over, I packed up to go home. The feeling of happiness was overwhelming! Everything was just so nice, meeting his family, seeing his niece perform, the conversations with no sexual motive. Just genuine!

A few days go by, and we started talking on the phone daily. We didn't text because his phone was as old as a dinosaur phone.

School was starting, my best friend Nat and I started our Dietary Aide course. It's a weekly course one class weekly for eighteen weeks! I was ready and couldn't wait to finish so I could better myself, in hopes to get a better job. I was so happy and realized that it was a breeze because I've worked in this line of work for quite some time before, without the college certification.

Being certified meant I could work in long-term care, which meant I could make decent money, compared to minimum wage. Depending on whether I get hired. I took my course, wrote the exams. All that fun stuff. Meanwhile I worked and dated Joey. I was so happy and busy.

This one particular evening, I was driving down the highway to his house, but my car does not have GPS. I got to a certain point and the road was blocked and it was nine at night. There had been a bad accident. I felt bad for the situation, but I had to reroute going down gravel side roads. After for driving 20 minutes out of my way I finally come up to a four corner stop and realized that if I turned right, it was just down the road in five minutes. I was so happy and relieved. I finally pulled into Joey's driveway. He has the house lit up like the Griswold's on National Lampoons Christmas Vacation so, I didn't miss it., *what a sweetie*!

I walked into his house, and he waited for me with a glass of red wine and told me the whirlpool was waiting. What, really ..*okaaaay*! I opened the bathroom door he had bubbles, candles, lights dimmed, the whole shebang! I get in the tub; he knocks on the door. He had a big smile and said to relax that he would be waiting for me. Wow! I was in the tub relaxing thinking, am I dreaming? This can't be real! I reach over press the button on the settings for the jets to come on. It's on for about five minutes and now the suds are overflowing…I'm laughing and yelling for Joey to come in and turn it off. I was afraid if I would stand up more water would overflow. He couldn't hear me because he was on the phone with one of his buddies and the music was blasting. I'm in the tub laughing so hard. He finally comes in and he was also laughing his ass off… that was such a great night to remember. We stayed up till 3 am and from that night on, I never left.

Work was continuing to be good, class was great, and I had my prince charming.

I had to do volunteer hours for my course. I did my thirty hours at a long-term care facility in the next town. They liked my personality so much they hired me on. I was so excited, now I had two jobs and all that I had wanted. I was so happy! When I was hired, I initially took a temporary part-time position.

During this period, I was occupied with my coursework, homework, two jobs, and spending time with my boyfriend. About a week later, we decided to make our relationship official. I was overjoyed. He was equally pleased and proud of me. Now that I was living outside of town, I made time to visit my mother, who would prepare supper for me on course nights. It was an ideal arrangement.

A few weeks later, Joey and I went out to a local bar. While we were having pre-drinks, we simultaneously said, "I have something to say.." and then we both expressed our love for each other at the same time, which brought us immense happiness and even tears of joy from Joey. I was now unbelievably happy; my heart felt full. This was genuine, not just empty words. I felt like I've met my angel. We go out with another couple for appetizers and drinks sometimes, and it is so much fun.

I felt unstoppable as I continued to improve myself and feel loved for being myself.

A few weeks passed, and I am invited to Joey's nephew's birthday supper at his parents' house, where I met his entire family. This includes about twenty people, his sisters, nieces, nephews, and his hundred-year-old grandmother. As an only child with just my mom and dad, this experience was new and special for me. Meeting so many people at once was overwhelming, but they genuinely enjoy my company, which helped to ease my anxiety. The experience was wonderful. I felt included and accepted without judgment.

Joey and I were progressing well. I applied for positions at various companies while completing my practicum. During my hours, I was hired full-time. I was ecstatic and immediately called Joey, who was very proud of me. My life felt amazing. I was finally where I need to be and with whom I belonged.

At nearly forty years old, I am truly happy. Through meeting all of Joey's friends and him meeting mine, I can confidently say that everything is fantastic, and my life is where it should be. Thanksgiving supper was beautiful, with eighteen of us around the table. I have never felt so thankful in my life. After the meal, I learned how to play euchre. My mother never had the patience to teach me card games, so this was a new and enjoyable experience for me. Although I am typically shy and afraid of making mistakes, I found joy in learning despite my initial lack of skill.

Months went by, and we soon celebrated my first birthday weekend together. Joey gifted me a Chicago Blackhawks jersey, my father's favorite team. This thoughtful gesture had brought me to tears of happiness. Feeling loved and respected was something I hadn't experienced in a long time. We celebrated my first Sunday birthday with his entire family and my mom, making it an unforgettable day. As the months passed, our love continued to grow. Christmas arrived, filled with beautiful family traditions such as attending Christmas Eve Mass, being included, and loved, feels wonderful.

Eventually, we became engaged and married. I have never felt so happy and accomplished in my life. I am employed full-time in a job I am passionate about, with benefits and vacation. I am deeply in love with my husband and living the life of which I have always dreamed.

I will never give up now, thanks to the love and support I receive every day, remembering that it's me that needed to love myself first for things to change. I want to extend my deepest gratitude to my incredible husband, who also helped to change my life and helped to show me that life is worth living.

Author notes:

My journey to self-love was anything but easy. For years, I had struggled with self-doubt, constantly seeking validation from others and placing my worth in the hands of external circumstances, despite the numerous obstacles that were, personal, emotional, and professional; that made me question my place in the world.

But through each setback, I slowly began to realize that the key to true happiness was *not* found in the approval of others, but in accepting and loving myself first.

It wasn't an overnight transformation; it took time, reflection, and a lot of inner work.

As I have embraced my worth and started living authentically, something incredible has happened, the right people, including my now-husband, entered into my life. I realize now that they were drawn to my confidence and sense of self, and together, those things created a life full of love, support, and understanding.

I hope that by sharing my story with you, others will be inspired to go on their own journeys of self-discovery and self-love. I believe that when you start by loving who you are, the world around you, shifts.

It's not about finding the right person or the perfect circumstances, it's about building a strong foundation of self-worth, first. I hope my message is clear: **when you invest in yourself and learn to love yourself fully, everything else will fall into place.**

I hope my story encourages others to take that first step toward self-love, as it's the catalyst for lasting change in life.

Until we meet again,

Sam Shaw

www.ingramcontent.com/pod-product-compliance
Lightning Source LLC
Chambersburg PA
CBHW051246120626
46547CB00014B/1810